WILLIAM WALLACE – A SCOTS LIFE is a serious yet easy-to-read short biography of one of Scotland's key historical figures.

The author has created an historically accurate and realistic portrait of the man in his time. Wallace is a hero, but one whose essential heroism is of a spiritual even more than a military kind.

William Wallace – a Scots life

WILLIAM WALLACE
A SCOTS LIFE

WILLIAM WALLACE

A SCOTS LIFE

GLENN TELFER

© Glenn Telfer
© Illustrations Tim Pomeroy

*First published
in Scots language version 1995
Reprinted 1995, 1996*

This edition 1998
Argyll Publishing
Glendaruel
Argyll PA22 3AE
Scotland

British Library Cataloguing-in-Publication Data.
**A catalogue record for this book is available from
the British Library.**

ISBN 1 874640 64 5

Origination
Cordfall Ltd, Glasgow

Printing
Caledonian International
Book Manufacturing, Glasgow

CONTENTS

Scots Legends Series

Scotland is a nation with a long history, a country made up of a variety of peoples, living lives in many different ways. There was a time not so long ago when things Scottish were regarded as a poorer form of life elsewhere. The Scots language for example was felt to be something which should be discarded at the first opportunity. Thankfully these attitudes are fast disappearing.

More than ever before, Scottish people now appreciate that the richness of their own history and language cannot be replaced by anything else. Our schools are reflecting these changed attitudes and now actively promote the Scots language.

The Scots Legends series is part of this new confidence in how we express ourselves and presents well-researched life stories of significant figures from past and present. Titles already produced on William Wallace, Robert the Bruce and the modern football coaching hero, Jock Stein have all been well received. Further titles are in planning.

The present book is an English language version of the book about William Wallace that first appeared in Scots in 1995. Demand from within Scotland, from England and from overseas for a standard English version compels us to comply. This is no diminution of the value of the Scots language version. Rather it is to meet the need for Scots history content, in whatever language, that is the force behind this book. The text follows the Scots version closely and can be used in parallel with it.

FOREWORD

Wallace lived in an age that was largely pre-literate. It is not surprising therefore that his name appears in only a few documents and letters. Added together, this information would scarcely fill a postcard. It contains few facts and nothing personal. What we want to know about Wallace was never written down in his time. And yet, Wallace's story, repeated in hundreds of books and the movie *Braveheart*, is packed full of detail and incident. Where did all these facts come from and how much truth is in them?

The source for most of Wallace's story is a 12,000-line epic poem called *Wallace*. It was composed by Blind Harry around 1470, more than 150 years after Wallace's death. In time, as Harry's *Wallace* became an old work, seemingly close to Wallace's own age, it increasingly came to be taken as an accurate version of his life. Of the many books on Wallace that have published, nearly all have Harry as their ultimate source.

Critical readers of Harry have surely always been aware that much of the tale is fanciful, but Harry's claim to have had access to a narrative written by a friend of Wallace has made it difficult to separate the wheat from the chaff. It was only with the publication of *Hary's Wallace* by Matthew McDiarmid in 1968 that we were able to see Harry's *Wallace* in its true light, a full-blooded nationalistic action adventure story. It is unlikely that Harry had access to any more concrete information on Wallace that we have now. The 'friend's manuscript' is a literary fiction. Certainly, Harry would have been able to draw on the story-telling and song tradition for extra tales about Wallace, but no story gains more in the telling than a war story. McDiarmid's scholarship shows that where Harry's version can be checked his facts are false and that other details in his tale follow narrative conventions of the day and cannot be considered true. Harry's *Wallace* is simply a creation of the imagination. And his poem should be considered as a fifteenth century equivalent of an action movie in the *Die Hard* or *Lethal Weapon* tradition. Its purpose was entertainment.

But Harry had a serious purpose too. This was to restore Wallace to his rightful place in the hearts of Scots. His work gives voice to our heartfelt need for a hero. And Scots need to remember who we are – need echoed in the popular reaction to the movie, *Braveheart*. Over the centuries Blind Harry and Mel Gibson can join hands in agreeing that it is the spirit of man that matters. I put my hand there too.

Glenn Telfer
Edinburgh
June 1998

A brave heart

Introduction

William Wallace . . . a brave heart
in a noble cause

In writing this I often found myself wondering what
attracted me to Wallace's story. I think the answer is
that it is in his story that Scotland's people first see
themselves clearly in history. And, at a time of guile
and empty talk among their leaders, Scots hear
somebody speaking simply and only for Scotland.
Whatever Wallace did, we know that he did it for his
country. That makes all the difference.

Wallace has no story separate from the story of

Scotland's long fight to retain her independence from England. We know nothing of his interests and private life, indeed, from the time that we first know of him he can scarcely have had any. From that moment when he drew his sword and struck down the English Sheriff of Lanark his whole life was spent in nothing but the service of his country.

In hard times he was a hard man. He was a man that had no time for the faint hearts and schemers in the Scottish camp. But he was also a man of honour and a realist who would have understood and sympathised with the tricky position of the great noble families of the land. And above all, he knew that you do not get the best from people by asking for less than they can give. Wallace asked the folk of Scotland and many gave their all. But if he expected much of them, he expected more of himself. Wallace stood by his principles to his bloody end. His vision of a free Scotland, his courage and loyalty, was shared by many in Scotland then. They knew, as he did, that the struggle would only be won by putting themselves on the line. It's a sacrifice that comes down to Scots now.

The War of Independence was a long time ago, but, in a way, it still continues; Scots distinctiveness as people, their relationship with England, their freedom from a sad past, all these things are not yet resolved. We look to the past, to the lives of men and women who stood for Scotland, to find some answers. Of course, they are hard to find. But sometimes, when looking to the past, you can feel a bit closer to some sort of answer about courage, loyalty and vision in the service of your country. With so many nowadays unsure about their feelings, Wallace tells us that it is a noble thing to care about Scotland.

Scotland Then

Our country, a magical and vast
land with God's stamp of freedom
marked all over it

Most of the world's countries are comparative
newcomers. Some, though, can be found far back in
time. Scotland is one such country. A thousand years
ago something closely resembling her can be seen
clearly, both in a geographical sense and in the minds
of her people. But Scotland did not just appear in a
snap of a finger. No, it took a lot of pain, truces and

treachery, hard hearts, courage, and most of all decent and hard working people to bring Scotland into being.

For numberless centuries, generation upon generation had struggled to win a living from the land. It was this never-ending cycle of daily graft that built Scotland out of the hard wilderness that was so much of our country. And it was this same day to day toughness that kept the land out of the hands of greedy or desperate people from other places. Yes, sweat and tears, the swing of a sword and spilt blood were the midwives of Scotland's birth.

Right from the beginning of their history, long before our story here, Scots found themselves jammed between big and unruly neighbours. There were the axe-wielding Vikings, only a boat ride over the North Sea, always on the lookout for land and booty. The Irish were not far away; cousins, it is true, but already well noted for being wild men always ready for a fight. Finally, there was England. Always interfering. Although at the time our story starts there had been no big war between the two countries within living memory, everybody knew that it was the ambition of every English prince to turn Scotland into the top part of England.

Now in those days you had to be always ready to defend yourself and your own. For if you were not, then someone would take everything from you. Over time, all this fighting, arguing and fist shaking made Scots into the sort of people that were not afraid to say, "These are my people. This is my land. I come from Scotland!"

The land then was their only larder and they were always on it. Working with it and working against it, fighting and dying for it. That is the way life was then. In the most direct way they were the land and it was them. The land called Scotland. Their country Scotland. We must remember we are talking about real people. Modern day Scots are their children.

But what was that country like then? What would be our impressions if we went back? The first thing we would notice is how quiet it was. The birds, the wind, the beasts, these would be the only noises that you would hear outside of someone's house. You would notice the freshness of the air, the reek of peat fires, the rich heavy smell of cattle. Scotland was a land of small settlements of farmers and keepers of cattle and sheep. There were some bigger towns and some big castles and churches, but most of Scotland was a land of so much empty space. It was a land of wild and lonely mountains and moors, lochs and woods and great forests. In these wild places lived deer, boars, wolves and, so people believed, spirits, goblins and fairies. It must have seemed a bigger place, more mysterious and magical. Scotland was, as it still is, beautiful.

But Scotland was also a hard land. Our ancestors had to work very hard indeed to survive. It was dangerous too. Disease and starvation were never far from their thoughts. Fierce animals roamed at will. Robbers could strike at any time. All the years of backbreaking toil could count for nothing if illness came or the crops failed or your sheep were stolen. People had a stronger sense of fate forcing itself on them than we have now. They also had a greater ability to endure whatever hardship came their way or the self-sufficiency to tackle it head on. They were made tough and resourceful. They were a proud people too, for everything they had they deserved. Especially their country's freedom.

People then saw and felt differently about lots of things from the way we do now. Their notions of what was useful or interesting was very different from ours. They knew about the land, having words for features that our modern eyes would not recognise. They knew about the ways of the beasts that they worked. They were interested in stories of their ancestors and the affairs of their masters, family and friends. Things that confused them, we can now explain with science. But, on the other hand, things that confuse us they would see clearly as the works of Heaven or maybe Hell. They could be just as sensible and just as daft as us.

And they believed above all in God and his will. They believed it with a depth and sincerity long lost to us. Their faith was the source of so much of their strength of character and amazing fortitude. They felt the benevolent presence of God in all that they did. It was their faith that gave meaning to their lives and to their deaths. And they were a people who knew how to die.

So much has changed since the time of our story. This can make us believe that people then were so

different from us. But they were not. We have their
eyes, their faces, their hair, their smiles and laughter,
their sense of fun and their temper. They were, as Scots
still are, a people made by the land and the weather.
Looking back over seven hundred years, despite the
changes in beliefs, opinions and lifestyle, Scottish people
see themselves. They are the children of that race.

Now, when it happened, the English invasion was
so terrible an event that most people were too afraid to
do anything. But there were others who, afraid though
they would be, thought that their duty to their friends
and country was a precious responsibility and spoke
up and said No! to invasion and injustice. It is these
people who give life to our story. People that loved their
country with all their hearts and would put themselves
on the line for it, come what may. Such a person was
William Wallace.

Not much at all is known of this man now. What we
can say for certain is that the idea of the kind of people
that Scots think they are owes much to those years of
war with England when Wallace was their leader. And
perhaps even the very existence of Scotland herself, as
we understand it, can be connected with this period of
her history.

A good student

And that completes what we know for sure about Wallace's early days and his family. The rest of the information we have comes from a long poem called *Wallace* written by Blind Harry about 170 years after Wallace died. People used to believe that the poem was mainly historical facts, but now we know that it's mainly fiction. Still, there may be some truth in it and it's all we have.

However, the absence of solid facts does not mean that we are left with nothing, for we can make some good assumptions based on our knowledge of the Scotland of his time. Compared with a modern biography we may find ourselves disappointed with the vagueness of this approach, but we must remember that every historical figure, as we understand them, is a creation of the imagination. In Wallace's story your sense of the person behind the bare bones of his story is dependent on your own imagination.

In Wallace's time few people had any schooling as we would understand it. And it would probably only be in his study of the Christian faith that we would recognise anything that would look like an actual school lesson. Nevertheless, although we cannot be sure about the details of his education, we can make good guesses as to the sort of things he would have learned. Wallace would have been taught all about his family history, legends with heroes and villains and stories of the spirit world; this was considered important knowledge in those days. Poetry and music were the main forms of entertainment and the ability to recite really long poems and to sing was highly regarded. The ability to do this well depended on great powers of memory, for nothing was written down to help you.

Certainly he would be taught practical things connected with his family's position as landowners; things to do with managing an estate, animals, tenants. One thing we can be certain that he learned was the martial arts; the use of sword, dirk and shield, bow and spear. Somehow it is easy to imagine him as a good student when it came to practising with his bow and arrow.

Wallace would have grown up probably speaking three languages equally well – Scots, Gaelic and French. The old version of the Scots tongue was the main language of Lowland Scotland in Wallace's day, but enough Gaelic might have been spoken to make knowing the two languages a necessity. Gaelic might have been the language of some of Wallace's relatives who lived in the north of the country. French was the first language of the nobility, as it was in England too, and anybody with connections to the nobility would naturally speak it. There can be no definitive answer to the question as to what was Wallace's preferred or first language, or even if he had one, but most experts agree that it was probably Scots.

Compared with our own times, in those days a person's job prospects were more limited. What you could do really depended on what your family did. As the youngest son, William would not necessarily have had great prospects ahead, but he could be assured of a comfortable, if modest, life. Traditionally, younger sons from the middle sorts of families went into the Church. This may well have been young Wallace's intended future for it is said by Blind Harry that he was educated by uncles who were priests, firstly at Dunipace near Stirling and later at Dundee. If this is true he would have been taught Latin and probably to read and write. This was a rare skill in those days.

We may wonder about the great strength of Wallace's love of his country and its liberty and ask where it came from. Blind Harry's poem tells us that while he was studying for the priesthood he was inspired by his uncle who told him the stories of all the brave people of olden times who fought and died for their country.

There may be some truth to this. For in those days the Scottish Church was fiercely patriotic and many priests were soon to be numbered among the unknown heroes of the coming war.

But the main part of your feelings for your country comes from your family and community. Now, Scotland then was a very tribal sort of place and Scots were very aware of the distinctions between them and other Scots – speech differences, differences in appearance and manner – but they were also aware of the common bond that united them. A bond of shared history and loyalty to land and king. A bond that had come from a distant past. Something Celtic in its origin. And first given shape by the Romans and their wall. Then later refined by the Celtic Church with its love for the land. This bond was greater than all the differences.

It was this sense of bond that Wallace was exposed to as a youngster. And not just Wallace. From the grandest to the poorest, man and woman, young and old, wherever they came from, Scotland's ancestors were to show that Wallace was not alone in his feelings for his country. As for his big heart, maybe one just as big is there inside us all.

What else do we know? Nothing! But as we know that man, so do we know the boy. He would have been sturdy, adventurous, a lover of action. We can easily see him playing at soldiers. He must have been a proud boy and brave too, one who would stand up for himself and for others. The sort of boy who would make a good, true friend. We can imagine him being rather too determined for his own good at times. He seems to me in lots of ways an unlikely person for a priest and, for Scotland at least, it's perhaps just as well that he did not become one.

weather on the night that he died. It was a bad, black night for Scotland in other ways too.

There was only one direct claimant to the throne of Scotland and that was the King's grand-daughter, Princess Margaret. Her father was the King of Norway. Although she was only three years old the little Princess from across the North Sea was made the Queen. A group of powerful nobles and churchmen, known as the Guardians, were appointed to rule the kingdom in her name until she was old enough to do it herself.

The major problem with the Princess was the question of who should marry her, for whatever family could arrange the match for their son would win Scotland. King Edward of England was naturally keen to promote his son as the ideal husband. In a treaty made in July 1290 he got what he wanted. King Edward had tried to get the negotiators for the Princess's marriage to surrender certain Scottish rights and laws, but they had totally refused to do this. He was not too concerned over this refusal, for Scotland would effectively come under English control when his son married Princess Margaret. It was not to be!

Within three months Princess Margaret was dead. King Edward's hopes for Scotland had come to nothing. It was not clear who would be the new king. Robert Bruce and John Balliol, two of Scotland's most powerful nobles, were the main contenders for the empty throne, but there were others in the contest. Each had a strong case for themselves and too many, it was feared, were prepared to put hand to sword when they said, "Me!"

It seemed as if a civil war was about to break out. The Bishop of Saint Andrew's wrote to King Edward and asked him to solve the problem by being an impartial judge and fairly looking at the case of each of the claimants and deciding by law who had the best claim. We do not know if everybody agreed to the Bishop writing to King Edward, or if they fully knew of it in advance, but once King Edward agreed there was no going back on it. If King Edward played fair there was some sense in him being the judge; he was one of the most powerful kings in Europe and nobody would argue with his decision. A civil war would be avoided.

It is at this point in our story that you find that English and Scottish historians often disagree. The English historians think that King Edward's intentions to the Scots were honest. The Scottish historians think that from the beginning he was seeking to undermine Scottish independence and hoping to create a situation in which he was the master of Scotland. Whatever his eventual intentions, from the beginning King Edward used his influence as judge to force the Scottish claimants to surrender certain parts of Scottish independence and to recognise him as their legal master. King Edward was insistent that the Kings of England were owed these rights. The Scots said that he was not. But King Edward got his way and forced the competitors for the Scottish throne to recognise him as their overlord. The Scots who protested at this were told that their opinion did not matter.

Finally, in November 1292, King Edward chose John Balliol, Lord of Galloway. This was a fair decision. Balliol was crowned King John the First of Scots. Even at the start of his rule not everyone was happy with Balliol as king. Some people because they had supported somebody else to be king. Others because Balliol had sworn an act of fealty to King Edward when he was at Newcastle. Now, what this meant was that Balliol agreed to recognise King Edward as the overlord, the real master, who was allowing Balliol to be king in his own country. The Scottish people were proud of their independence – they did not like what Balliol had done. But most people also knew that Balliol had little choice over the act of fealty. King Edward was just too powerful to be opposed in this matter.

The Scots did not have to wait long before King Edward started acting the part of overlord – interfering with the governing of Scotland, the church, decisions made in the Scottish courts, telling King John what to do. Poor King John was finding out the real price of being picked by King Edward. He was starting to look like a puppet. Many Scots felt that the dignity of Scotland was being lessened by King Edward's bullying and by King John giving in to him.

Now, King Edward at this time was involved in a war with the French. He told King John that he wanted help from Scotland. He felt that he had the right to do this because he was the overlord. The Scots had no quarrel with the French. They made it clear to King John that they were sick of being pushed around by King Edward and had no intention of helping him in his war with the French. Under this pressure King John said that he would not help King Edward and immediately made a defence treaty with France. Everybody knew that King Edward would be furious. Scotland prepared for war with England.

Perhaps King John thought that he could unite Scotland behind him and that King Edward would be too busy with his problems in France to want to fight the Scots. Perhaps he hoped that he and King Edward could come to some new arrangement that would avoid a war and get the English king off Scotland's back. But King John's hopes and intentions came to nothing for King Edward was not a man to meddle with. He rushed back from France with his army with the intention of teaching the Scots a lesson. The Scots struck first and invaded the North of England. Their campaign was ineffective and they had retreated home by the time King Edward's army arrived. The English totally destroyed Berwick upon Tweed. It was said that every single person found in the town was killed.

News of the atrocity fired the Scots, revenge was

on their minds. The chance for it came very soon. At Dunbar they let their hearts rule their minds and so flew into the English. That glorious charge of the wild Scots did not panic the English soldiers. They had done a fair share of fighting in the previous years against the Welsh and the French. They had the experience and the resolve to cope with it. It was soon all over. Totally defeated, the Scots fled before the advancing victorious English army.

King Edward chased King John half way up Scotland. The Scottish king knew that it was all over for him and finally surrendered his kingdom. King Edward made him apologise on his knees lots of times in different places just so the Scots would know who was the master now.

After setting up things in Scotland as he wanted them King Edward went home. But he did not go home empty handed. He took King John as hostage and all sort of valuable things from Scotland. Included among the booty was a large slab of stone that the Kings of Scotland had always been crowned upon, the Stone of Destiny. It was a powerful symbol of Scots independence. Before King Edward left he made all kinds of important people promise to recognise him as their master and he made them sign their names as proof of this. This list of names is called the Ragman Rolls. The name of Wallace is not on it.

King Edward went back home to his plans for

war with France. He left behind him all the soldiers and officials he needed to run Scotland as part of England. Five years after being asked to help the Scots reach an agreement on their new king, he was their king!

Nobody knows what Wallace was doing during this period. But knowing how Wallace felt about his country he would certainly have wanted to fight the English. There is a good chance, then, that he was with the Scots Army and took part in the shameful retreat after their defeat. He would have realised then that a conventional war was out of the question for the English were too powerful. He would also have known that many of the Scots nobles were in two minds about supporting any further resistance to King Edward for they were afraid of losing their land and titles. Resistance would have to come from people whose duty to their country was clear to them and uncomplicated by circumstances. People who were prepared to live as outlaws and strike at the enemy's weak spots. This would be no war of grand knights and waving banners; no, this would be long, hard and dirty. Ambushes, raids, destruction of English property and assassination would be the only way to wear down the English.

The war was hardly over when resistance to King Edward's new rule sprang up. Who were these people who dared to go against King Edward? Some would have been soldiers from the defeated Scots Army who wanted another try, some would have been people who had a personal grudge against the English as a result of the bad things that had been happening, but most would be the ordinary people we have spoken of who just loved their country and wanted it to be free.

But we must remember that freedom's cause was not just served by the men that carried the spear, for a war is not won only by fighting. The people in the background are just as important. From the brave churchmen who worked to unite support for the struggle at home and abroad to the wife who shared her roof and her food with the Scots resistance. They were all patriots.

the murder of the Sheriff

and his men slew Haselrigg and his staff. This was a major blow against English domination and is the first time we have concrete proof of Wallace in history. The town would have been in uproar. Outraged and afraid, the English could see that the rebellion had taken a new turn for the worse. Away from English eyes a few celebrations would have been the order of the day; the Sheriff and his staff cut down! You can imagine the effect of this on the morale of the Scots freedom fighters.

Exactly how it was done we cannot say. Blind Harry's poem has Wallace seeking revenge for the murder of Mirren Bradefute, his wife or wife to be, by Haselrigg. He has the Sheriff's assassination taking place in the middle of the night. After wiping out the guards, Wallace kicked in Haselrigg's door.

Haselrigg cried out, "Who's making all that noise?"

"Wallace!" our hero shouted. "The man you're looking for!"

You can almost feel the fear running up Haselrigg's back at these words. He tried to escape from Wallace into the safety of the darkness but his time had come. Wallace split his head down to the collar bone with a single swing of his sword and then dragged him down the stairs where he was stabbed again just to make sure. Haselrigg's house was then put to the torch.

Can you imagine the scene in the street that night? Houses burning, horses panicking, groups of men with torches and bloody weapons, clash of sword on sword, a swish followed by a dull thump as an arrow finds its target, curses and dogs barking, people crying out with fear in their voices, shouting, "What's happening, what's happening?"

But no matter how fanciful Blind Harry's version is, it certainly conveys the bold and violent nature of the deed. We must also remember that the killing of the Sheriff had to be a carefully planned operation. The Sheriff did not need to be told that he was a marked man; he would have a bodyguard. These would have to be dealt with – Wallace could not just rush in and give him the blade. Careful planning backed up with boldness was to be the way that Wallace did things.

Wallace was not the only one resisting English rule. By the time of Haselrigg's slaying the English authorities were having a hard time keeping the lid on what was a country-wide rebellion. We are not sure how it was organized or who, if anybody, was planning it all.

The English, though, were in no doubt as to the ultimate cause of the problem. They blamed the Scottish Church for encouraging the rebels. And in this they would not have been far from the truth, for the support of the Church was absolutely crucial. With many of the nobles in two minds about what to do, it was the Church that gave the rebellion credibility and the rebels unflinching support. And the rock at the centre of the Church, one of the country's greatest patriots, was Robert Wishart, the Bishop of Glasgow.

It is also clear that the rebellion was not the creation of the Scottish Church. The real source of the rebellion was to be found in the hearts of men and women all over Scotland.

A Tough Man

That sword swing against
Haselrigg made Wallace
Scotland's most wanted outlaw
and its natural leader

We should not be surprised that we do not know anything about Wallace's movements before Haselrigg's killing. In those days people did not write things down the way that they do now. People remembered events through stories, poems and songs. These have been lost to history for a long time now.

Only Blind Harry's poem gives us stories of Wallace before Haselrigg's killing. He has Wallace, assisted by his close friends, Gray, Kerlie and Stephen of Ireland, avenging insults and meeting the challenge of arrogant English strongmen and sword champions. The English and traitorous Scots are hacked down at every opportunity. Woman, children and priests are the only folk of English blood that are spared the blade.

But the Wallace of Blind Harry's tale is too easily ruled by fiery emotions, too reckless to lead men. The hard canny survivor with nerves of steel and an iron will that was the real Wallace would not have risked himself or his forces in the way that Blind Harry's poem leads us to believe. But we do not make the real Wallace any less heroic by saying that these stories are tall tales. Wallace did not become the leader of rebels by being a timid sort. He required great personal courage, great physical toughness, great audacity and great strength of spirit; all the qualities of a real hero.

Danger and hardship were the rebels' constant companions. The Scottish rain running down the back of your neck, the cold winds, damp leather, wet feet, a frosty morning's wakening with stiff bones on the hard earth. The fireless camp with only a stone to suck to hold back the rumble of your belly, the poor horses having only the hard iron of the bridle for their sustenance. The odd sound that makes your heart race and has you fitting an arrow to the bowstring. There is no romance in this life inside a stinking suit of chain mail. Hearing kind words and warning of danger from people, but at the same time searching their eyes for the traitor's smile.

The hours in the saddle, the hours of watching and waiting, the terrible tension of the wait. And then, the rush of arrows. An ambush! The dirt and blood mixed freely in hand-to-hand combat. Sword on sword, axe against spear, the frantic search for another crossbow bolt, the spilt blood on the earth. No opportunity was overlooked to punish the English and their Scottish supporters – cut them down wherever they are, burn their castles, steal their money and supplies! You had to be a hard man for this sort of thing. Wallace showed that he was the master at it.

Now, people then were not any more heartless or cruel than at any other time in history. And before the war the English and Scottish people had not been enemies. But this war of invasion and resistance was, by its very nature, exceptionally cruel and people's hearts were quickly hardened.

In a mad feast of violence, Scottish resistance and English domination grew ever bigger and more cruel by feeding off each other. Lakes of tears filled on both sides of the border were proof that the Scot and the Englishman were evenly matched in cruelty and depravity. There was no surrender, there were no prisoners. Anyway, having but a small force and no fixed base, Wallace could not take prisoners even if he wanted too. If you were captured you would expect to be given the chop. And, yes, you would be!

As the news of Haselrigg's killing spread, the rebellion against the English was given a massive boost. Wallace became the most famous man in Scotland. People flocked to join him. Soon Wallace was leading a large body of rebels on horseback. Wallace and the other rebels in different parts of the country were not yet ready to face the might of England on the battle field. So the guerilla tactics continued. Wallace would attack the English and cause as much trouble as he could and then ride away before they could bring along extra soldiers. To fight this sort of war you have to be constantly on the move and you have to know what the enemy is doing. You need, above all, the support of the people. The Scottish people supported the rebels, no doubt quietly at first, and as the rebellion grew in strength and confidence, then more openly. When Wallace joined up with Andrew Murray, who led the rebellion in the North-East, it was all over for the English. Outside of Berwick and some castles they had no power left by the summer of 1297. The government of Scotland was back in the hands of Scots. What would King Edward do next? Few were in any doubt!

THE NOBLES
AND THE ENGLISH

**Many Scottish nobles supported
the rebellion, but did so secretly –
they feared punishment from
King Edward**

While Wallace was fighting most of the nobles and
powerful men in Scotland had been pretty quiet. The
hard lesson they had been taught at the Battle of
Dunbar did not need repeated. Some of the nobles
supported Wallace, but secretly. They were still afraid
of the English king.

Perhaps they were inspired, and probably a bit
ashamed too by Wallace's example. Perhaps they were
also afraid that if Wallace was successful then they
would be left out of things. For if Scotland won back

her independence then the powerful nobles would be the ones that had helped in that fight and who had commanded the successful army. So, taking advantage of the turmoil that summer, they decided to have another crack at the English and they created an army out of their followers and tenants.

Wallace must have been pleased by this for the Scottish cause took a big leap forward. King Edward would be pleased too, for this rebellion of the nobles was the sort of situation that he could deal with. An army was quickly sent to Scotland.

The Scottish nobles met the English army at Irvine. But, seeing once more their old conquerors returned, the fear of death was put into the Scottish hearts and they decided to negotiate with the English instead of fighting. To the immortal shame of their country the Scots nobles finally surrendered to the English on 7th July. The Scottish nobles rebellion was over. Never had the English won a battle so cheaply and never had the Scots lost so much pride in defeat – and not a man with so much as a blister to show for it. We can imagine the cruel jests in the English camp that night. But unknown to those same English soldiers was the fact that the true Scottish thistle had not been trampled down by their parade of strength.

If Wallace had been pleased at first by the nobles rebellion he would have been frustrated and bitterly disappointed at the end of it. But, perhaps, not entirely surprised by it. The surrender by the nobles proved to Wallace, Murray and the other patriots that they could not rely on their country's normal leaders. For the present, they would have to do it alone.

But some good had come out of this disappointing event. For the English had been tied down at Irvine while the surrender negotiations were going on. This left Wallace free from interference to build and train the Scottish army. The English were in no doubt that the Scottish nobles deliberately strung out the surrender negotiations for this very purpose.

The people who joined Wallace in the forests of Selkirk that summer knew the justice of Scotland's cause and felt a strong sense of duty to their country. But it was Wallace's spirit that turned these feelings into the courage to stand against the mighty English on the field of battle. It was spirit that turned individual beliefs into a collective will that said, "Let's do it!"

For Wallace to create an army to fight for Scotland at the same time as the country's normal leaders had abandoned that same fight because of the presence of a more powerful enemy was truly a great achievement.

It's easy now to be hard on the Scots who surrendered at Irvine and left the fight to Wallace. Most of them loved their country but felt that their hands were tied. The leaders of this rebellion, you must remember, were rich and titled. They had a lot to lose if they drew a sword against King Edward again. And seeing the tough, experienced English knights made them think again and decide that perhaps the time was not yet right after all. Not all of them felt this way, but those in favour of the fight were voted down by the more cautious and the more afraid.

Meanwhile, in the Forest of Selkirk, the people who were disappointed with those who said, "Not me", and "Not this time", were going to Wallace.

"This time for Scotland!" "Ay, me!" They were the ancestors of modern Scots, they were ordinary people and at the same time heroes.

STIRLING BRIDGE

The English victory at Irvine was
an empty one for they did not
gain any control of the country
and they had not addressed
themselves to the big problem –
Wallace

By August 1297, Wallace had cleared Fife and
Perthshire of English rule and, joining up with Andrew
Murray who had liberated the north and east, was
besieging Dundee Castle. It was clear to the English
that Wallace had to be beaten in battle or made to
surrender. And it had to be done soon before he took all
the castles and towns out of English hands.

The English army advanced to Stirling. Wallace and

Murray's force marched over to meet them there. The days of the guerilla fighting were over. It was time to take their freedom back. There was only one way to do this; destroy the whole basis of the English authority in Scotland, the English army. Also, if the Scots were to get any help from their European neighbours they would have to prove to them that their claim of independence was credible and that they were determined to stay free. The only way to do this would be to expel the English by force of arms.

The 9th of September found the two armies at Stirling and ready for a fight. Now, at this point some of the Scots nobles turned up and offered to negotiate some deal between the Scots and the English. These Scots nobles did not want to see a massacre of the Scots soldiers. They were really on the Scots side, but as we know, they were too afraid of King Edward to give Wallace obvious support. They wanted to reach an agreement similar to the one at Irvine. Also, perhaps, once more, they were wasting time to help extra Scots turn up for the coming battle, if it was to come to a battle.

Wallace and Murray, you can imagine, were not in favour of talking. There had been enough of that at Irvine. The English gave the Scots a last chance to surrender on the morning of the 11th.

Wallace's reply, "Tell your commander that we are not here to make peace, but to do battle and to defend ourselves and liberate our kingdom. Let them

come on and we shall prove this in their very beards."
So it was to be a battle then.

The armies were divided by the River Forth. The English were on the same side as the town and the castle. The Scots were on the other side, on the high ground called Abbey Craig, where the Wallace Monument is now. They had about 5,000 soldiers, nearly all of them spearmen. The English army had perhaps twice that number, including lots of cavalry. The English were confident – after all, only a month before they had scared another Scottish army into surrender. And they had an even lower opinion of the Scottish army that faced them now, calling them rogues and thieves.

Some of the English urged caution in going over the bridge which separated the two armies, but Cressingham, one of King Edward's governors in Scotland and one of the army commanders, was keen to get the fight over with as soon as possible. And the most direct route to the Scots was by the bridge. He insisted on his army using it, perhaps fearing that too much time spent readying his army would allow the Scots to retreat.

Like Wallace, Cressingham was anxious to settle the problem of who ran Scotland. As Cressingham saw it, there had been too much time wasting, and all at King Edward's expense. The Scots were just over the bridge – "Get over there and into them before they change their minds like at Irvine." A thumping victory

Stirling Bridge

would be a perfect end to a frustrating summer.

Cressingham had not realised that he was dealing with a completely different set of Scots entirely. So the English soldiers crossed the bridge.

Then, just when a certain number of English had assembled on the Scots side, the Scots flew down the hill and into them. It was just as some of the experienced English soldiers had feared would happen.

Things happened very quickly now. The English cavalry could not operate with all the sticky mud and puddles of the river bank. Soon the Scottish spears drove them into the river. Extra knights could not get over the bridge to help their comrades. And then, whether from the weight of all the men and horses, or due to Wallace having it weakened beforehand, the bridge collapsed. So that meant that the English on the Scots side were trapped. It was to the death now.

We can guess their feelings, for they would have known their fate. The mass of Scottish spearmen pushed forward. The English at the sharp end were killed, the ones at the back were shoved into the water and, with all the weight of armour, drowned. The Scottish archers fired their arrows into the middle of the struggling mass, causing even more confusion. Any English that tried to escape along the banks of the river were chopped down by Scottish infantry.

What a mess it was. The Scottish cries of triumph mingled with the curses and pleas of the defeated English and the fearful whinnying of their horses.

The English on the safe side of the river, seeing what had happened, fled for Berwick. However, those who did not have horses were wiped out by the Scottish nobles who, seeing how things had gone, finally decided to come in on the Scots side. Many of the English casualties that day occurred after the battle. Fleeing, disorganised and lost soldiers make easy victims. What had started as a battle, ended as a massacre.

It was a great day for the Scots army, for Wallace and Murray their commanders, for Scotland. English losses were very great and it meant the end of any possibility of the English regaining control of the country. It was not often that foot soldiers beat knights on horseback. It says much about the quality of leadership and courage that this army of mainly common folk could take on and beat professionals.

Stirling Bridge was a great and significant battle. It was the confidence booster that the Scots cause needed. It proved to Scotland's supporters abroad that the Scots were resolved and able. Scots losses were relatively light and only a bad injury to Murray had potentially serious implications for the cause. Despite the deaths and injuries, there was much to celebrate. All the planning, the hardship, the uncertainty of the dark days since the Battle of Dunbar had been put right – the English had got their just desserts.

INTO ENGLAND

A battle was over, but the war
was still to be fought

The Battle of Stirling Bridge made Wallace both the
saviour and the leader of his country. His authority
could not be denied by anyone and he did not waste
time by being falsely modest about what he had done.
Nor did he shirk from the enormous task that had so
suddenly come to him.

A special committee of nobles and bishops made him
and Andrew Murray the Guardians of Scotland. This
made their authority legitimate. One of their first

decisions concerned the army. It was still ready for action and eager for revenge. After the celebrations, Wallace took the army to Berwick and recaptured it. Murray had to be left behind as his injury was too serious. Wallace then started his preparations for his next plan; the invasion of England. By October they were ready. He wanted to teach the English a lesson they would not forget in a hurry.

And what a lesson! Nothing human it seemed could stop Wallace's victorious Scots army as it swept through the North of England. The soldiers took a cruel revenge on the English people. Those that did not escape were put to the sword. Anything that could be stolen was stolen, anything that could be burned was soon in flames. It was bad luck to be English that autumn.

King Edward was over the sea in Flanders with his army and Wallace had destroyed the other English army at Stirling, so the English people were totally defenceless. The only thing that they could do was pray. So they got down on their knees and prayed to one of their local saints – he was called Saint Cuthbert. It was supposed to be him that sent the terribly cold weather that near froze the Scots to death.

It was clear to the Scots army what to do. It was time to go home. It was November by this time anyway. Winter was on them and everybody wanted to be at their own fire. They would have lots to tell. It had been a long year.

For Wallace, though, we can be sure that there was no sitting around a fire telling of his successes in the war. There was much to be done if Scotland was to keep her newly won freedom. And Wallace would have to do it all alone for Murray had died while the army was sacking England. Wallace was now the sole Guardian.

The task of Guardian was one that demanded more than military genius. But not for Wallace the chance to ease into the task. In a space of six months he had come from being an unknown outsider in the great events of the time to being in the position of supreme power in his own country. Suddenly all that responsibility was his. It was a task that demanded great boldness of spirit as well as intelligence. One wrong decision and who could tell what would happen?

Wallace would have to finance and train the army. He would have to keep friends with other countries who might help us. He would have to encourage the nobles in Scotland to join the fight and, if they did join up, keep them from bickering among themselves. For it never took much to get the Scots nobles to draw daggers on each other.

Bringing the Scots together to face a common foe was the hardest task. Then, like now, Scots found it hard to all chip in together and forget their differences for the common good. Wallace had the Church and the common people behind him, but some of the really big nobles were still in two minds. Basically, they did not want to side with Wallace only to get beaten by King Edward the next year. Also, some of them were not pleased at the idea of a man of relatively humble birth running the country. The fact that Wallace had recently been made a knight and was now Sir William hardly made any difference to this feeling. But most of these nobles were quiet about their misgivings, for Wallace was very much in charge.

King Edward contemplates the problem of the Scots

IN POWER

1297 ended with Scotland free
once more

It had been a momentous year. At the New Year party there must have been some wild celebrating. But behind all the toasts and cheers there was a dark and fearful shadow lurking. And King Edward of England was in it. He would be back.

Wallace knew that the present liberation of Scotland would be a temporary thing. King Edward would have to be defeated more decisively than at Stirling Bridge and the English people punished more severely than the recent terrible Scottish raid on the North of England for the King to give up the prize of Scotland. The only way to do this was by showing a tremendous unity and standing together. Everything depended on this. The creation of this unity was Wallace's great task as Guardian of our country.

Looking back it might seem to us that unifying the country would not be a great problem. After all, very few Scots were sympathetic to the English King's desire to incorporate their country into England, even the fence-sitters and collaborators. But life then was more complicated than it may seem. People then did not live in a time of simple choices. We look back on the bare bones of history and miss all the subtle forces that animated our ancestors' lives. But although we cannot see these forces, we can imagine them; personalities, opinions, obligations to friends and relatives, a whole universe of ideas about fate, justice and honour unknown to us – these are what lie behind the choices Scotland's ancestors were faced with.

They were just as tied up in politics, just as stubborn in their own ideas about what was right and just as concerned to watch out for their family and friends as we are today. It is these easy-to-understand human feelings that lay behind what can seem like an incredibly complicated situation. Oh, and one more thing. If you made a bad choice, you could pay for it with your life.

The Scottish nobility were the group most

constrained by circumstances. For a start many nobles had estates and relatives in England and some probably considered themselves as members of a ruling elite rather than Scots or English as such. Others would have considered themselves like dual citizens and would be sickened at the thought of choosing an allegiance. Many were confused.

Aware of the pressures that would force the Scots nobles to oppose him, King Edward had taken hostages, mainly sons and daughters, just to make sure the nobles would not change their minds. Then there was the background politics to consider – who would be the King of Scotland.

Not everyone wanted King John back, especially the Bruce family who had long harboured hopes of winning the throne. A lot of the humming and hawing was about this – should the Bruces and all their supporters fight for Scotland and to hell with the consequences? Should they take the lead in the fighting or stay in the background? Should they fight to help King John win the Scottish throne back. Should they stay friendly with King Edward in the hope that he, or the next English king, would give them the Scottish Crown? There could be no easy answers to these questions for the Bruces.

All the noble families in Scotland were ultimately roped into the Bruce versus King John question. The nobles were for Scotland alright, but perhaps not if it meant that old rivals might end up better off. And there was a fear too that if King John came back he might want to punish those who had not done all that they could for him.

You can appreciate the difficult position of the nobles. Despite the Scots successes, the reality was that King Edward would be back. He was famous for never giving up. If the nobles went against him they risked losing all. Freedom of conscience for the nobles was to be bought at a high price – the loss of estate, fortune and, most important of all, the failure to satisfy their lordly obligations to their dependents and peers. The nobles were not really all that free to follow their hearts as you might think. In the years that followed the war, many have found it easy to criticise the nobles as a duplicitous and cowardly bunch, but such criticism does not take fully into account the political and cultural background.

It is in his work as our Guardian that we see another side of Wallace, one that is often overlooked, his intelligence. It's obvious that nobody could even consider tackling this task without a subtle mind and great organisational skills. It was an endless, exhausting task. Sorting out the army, receiving intelligence reports, news from abroad, organising meetings, making plans. He was not a man to mince his words and you might imagine that some of the faint hearts in our struggle were more afraid of him than of King Edward. In hard times Wallace did not back away from using hard words. And some of those that were in two minds about joining the Scottish cause must have been persuaded that bit more with the thought that their heads might well be looking out from a basket if they went against Wallace. This was no job for a sword-wielding muscleman (although Wallace was certainly that as well). This was a juggling act of the greatest complexity.

Scotland's different regions supported many different families and clans and races of people. Often they looked different and spoke separate languages. Even when all these different Scots agreed, bringing them together and working out a common plan was a very difficult thing to do. The forces that made Scotland strong – the independence of spirit, the hardiness, the loyalty to family and friends, the willingness to fight and that wild streak – were the selfsame forces that could blow it apart. It required diplomatic skills of great subtlety and much ruthlessness to keep the Scots united.

Wallace was intimately aware of the obligations, deals, understandings and rivalries that both held the country together and threatened to pull it apart. Nobles, churchmen, burghers, chiefs and lairds, the common people in all their wild diversity, had to be kept on the same path. This called for an instinctive feel for when to push softly with a point and when to force it. Wallace would need the common touch. But he would also need the ability to deal with the nobles on an equal footing without offending the codes of behaviour that governed a meeting between aristocrats and anyone else.

During this period Wallace must have been

practically living in his saddle. We can picture him and his friends riding over a landscape of snow. All wrapped up in enormous riding capes. Breath frozen in the air. Swords always handy, just in case. We can imagine the strain, the tiredness, the uncertainty taking its toll. We can see him in great halls, with his back to a roaring fire, debating whether the Pope was going to come out in favour of the Scots.

The greatness of Wallace is proven during this time. For he had great power and would have been able to do favours for his friends and kin, fill his pockets with gold and silver and, it was a real possibility, negotiate a surrender with King Edward and do well for himself out of it. Nobody can tell how they would stand up to the temptation of such power. And many a good man just would not be able to resist the chance of doing themselves a favour.

One thing we can be sure of is that if Wallace had abused his power then we would have heard of it – the English would have made sure of that! Wallace served just one cause; Scotland's and her rightful king. He was always careful to say so in all his letters and statements.

Even more extraordinary is how Wallace was able to command so effectively and inspire so many. For neither by birth nor by training had he been prepared for it. The source of Wallace's abilities will ever be unknown. For the harder one tries to understand greatness the more of a mystery it becomes. Perhaps we've all got the courage and vision and faith somewhere within ourselves. Wallace was just able to find it at the right time.

Crisis followed crisis. All Wallace could hope for was to keep the cause moving forward and keep the country from collapsing into a civil war. More than anyone Wallace had pulled us back from the brink of national suicide, but we have to remember the others too who stood with him. The hard, hard men of the original resistance gangs that did the cruel sword work that started the ball rolling. The thousands of people that did care about Scotland and her freedom and took up spear to prove it. The men and women who could not fight, but gave the rebels succour at a time when to do so could get you your hand, or even head, cut off. The nobles who put aside the complications of their position and flung themselves into the cause. And the brave men of the Church who showed the future that spirit was more than something the Church just preached about.

What these people were risking became evident by the summer of 1298. King Edward had come back from Flanders and was personally set on sorely punishing the Scots. He was an angry man.

The Battle of Falkirk

THE BATTLE OF FALKIRK

When King Edward came home
from France he immediately
set about planning
the invasion of Scotland

King Edward formed a big army which contained many
knights and archers, both of which the Scots were very
short of. He had arranged for the army to be supplied
by ships dropping off provisions along the coast. By July
1298 he was at Roxburgh and ready to begin the
punishment.

The English marched through the Borders and
Lothians destroying everything that they could lay their
hands on. But they found no people, for they all had

fled. Neither was the Scots army anywhere to be seen.

Wallace was being cautious. He knew that he must keep his army intact. If there was no Scots army then there was no independence. Wallace did not want to needlessly risk all our gains in a pitched battle with a superior enemy force. A pitched battle was just what the English were hoping for. Also, a good general does not sacrifice his own people if he can help it and, we must remember, the Scots army really was Wallace's people in the most direct sense. If Wallace's strategy could force the English to go home having achieved nothing but burning down houses, then King Edward had failed. Scotland would still be free, still have a strong army, and would still be in a good position for negotiating the return of King John and other Scots captured after the Battle of Dunbar.

This absence of the enemy caused many of the English soldiers to get very tense and frustrated. To make matters even worse the ships proved unreliable in supplying the army. The soldiers were getting hungry, very hungry. By the time the grand English army was at Kirkliston, near Edinburgh, it was in a bad way, being hungry and demoralised. The Welsh archers in the English army had fallen out with some of the English soldiers and fist fights had broken out between them. King Edward was forced to consider retreating to Edinburgh where he would start a general withdrawal from Scotland. Wallace's strategy was working. Without having to fight he was sending the English home defeated.

But Wallace was not content to see them go home without a 'souvenir' of their stay. An open battle was perhaps foolish, but a night attack on the English camp? At night the English advantages would be reduced; the archers would not have clear targets and the cavalry could not operate at all.

It was good idea. But it was betrayed. Two Scottish Earls, Dunbar and Angus, who sided with King Edward, had a spy who reported the Scottish plans. King Edward took his chance to sort out his disasterous Scottish campaign. If he could turn the tables on the Scots, make a surprise march to their camp and force them to battle then all might yet end well. With great haste he set off for the Scots camp at Falkirk.

His plan foiled and the English nearby, Wallace's options were reduced. The arguments of the hot heads, who all along had wanted to fly into the English, could not be resisted now. They were not afraid, in fact, quite the opposite. They had done the impossible at Stirling, why not again? Besides, they would have argued, if they did not deal the English a heavy blow now, they would just come back next year. Here and now it had to be decided who was in charge. There was a sense of resignation about Wallace's words to his army.

"I have led you to the ring. Dance if you can!"

It was the 22nd of July, 1298.

It was not an ideal situation for the smaller Scots army, but they were well-trained, well-motivated and Wallace was their leader. Four schiltroms or groups of spearmen had been formed. The men put on their helmets and took their places. Let the English come on!

The battle started when the English heavy cavalry charged the Scots spearmen. In seconds the thunder of the galloping horses became the crash of metal on metal, the whine of crippled horses, loud and fearful cries. Can you imagine the shock of the impact running up the shaft of the long Scots spears and hear the crack of them splintering. Some bodies would slither in a trail of blood all the way up the shaft. Battle had been joined. Knights would be thrown from their horses, horses would collapse sending groups of spearmen tumbling like skittles. The English cavalry would have made a big dent in the Scots formation, but it held. And then, after a struggle, drove the knights away. The close approach of the English cavalry to the position of the Scots cavalry led them to flee the field. The Scots cavalry, made up almost completely of nobles and their men, were never seen again that day.

Now when the English cavalry retreated after failing to break up the schiltroms, King Edward sent up his archers. Their job was to shoot down the schiltroms. This should have been the time that the Scots cavalry charged into the archers to prevent this happening. But we know that their cavalry had, by plan or cowardice or incompetence, betrayed their own side. So, without hindrance, thousands upon thousands of arrows poured through the sky and fell on the packed ranks of spearmen in the schiltroms. And when the deadly stream finally stopped, the English knights charged back into the thinned-out ranks.

It was obvious what would happen. The certainty of death would give their courage a reckless quality – "We're deid, lads. So sell your life dear!" Shot with arrows and hacked down by cavalry, they fought on to their bloody end. Not all the nobles fled the field. Some stayed with the ordinary soldiers and met their fate. The only Scots that we know of by name who were killed at Falkirk were those nobles. The names of the countless others are forever unknown, but not lost, for they live on in their children, the Scots of today.

Towards the end Wallace was dragged from the field raging with anger at the betrayal by the Scots cavalry and with sorrow at the loss. No matter how he felt about it, he could not be allowed to die at Falkirk. Scotland still needed him. Many others escaped as best they could. Wallace's force was hotly pursued by English cavalry. Even here he could strike back. We are told that Sir Brian le Jay and some other knights were led into a bog by the Scots. While they were floundering about, Wallace turned around and personally killed le Jay.

But despite these paybacks there was no denying that the English had won a tremendous victory. Pleased though King Edward would have been with the victory, it was obvious that the campaign had failed to meet its objectives. Scotland had not been recaptured, English authority had not been restored and Wallace and his forces were still at large. King Edward was to discover, as Wallace had done the year before, that winning a battle does not always solve the problem.

After Falkirk

The days following Falkirk were
very dark ones. Would the country
go to King Edward now?

Wallace must have been thrown into despair, flashed
with anger and frustration. Many a strong man or
woman would not have been able to take the pressure
of these days following the battle. Wallace, though, had
to shake off these feelings for he had practical things
that still had to be done.

Certainly the English had given the Scots a
whipping, but their spirit had not been crushed. The
Scottish resistance had not collapsed. Scots still ran

the country. More than ever, Wallace's presence was needed to help them stand firm.

The big question was, what was King Edward to do now? He had a big army to feed and pay, he could not keep them in Scotland forever. He must have hoped to scare the Scots into surrendering? Could he? Would they? The answer was no. In fact, over the coming months resistance to him got greater.

Well, if he could not win Scotland by force of arms, he would try a bit of diplomacy. If King Edward could get Wallace to surrender with all his men and their supporters in the Church, then surely the Scottish resistance would collapse. Only a few wild men would be outside the peace process if Wallace surrendered and they could easily be hunted down and dispatched.

So King Edward offered Wallace his 'peace'. This meant that he would forgive Wallace for fighting with him and probably give him a reward as well, if Wallace would recognise King Edward as his lord and promise never to rebel again. This was an honourable offer and not many would have been able to resist the temptation to both save face and come out of it well-off. Wallace could have negotiated a pardon for his men too, for King Edward could be generous in victory when it suited him. Wallace and his supporters would keep their lives and Scotland would be a region of England. You can guess Wallace's reply to the offer. A free Scotland was the only prize he wanted.

When King Edward heard of the rejection he must

have known at once that he was dealing with a different type of man. One that stood by his beliefs through good and bad, one that was not secretly looking out for himself, one that could not be bought with gold or titles – a rarity in any age.

Now, commoners like Wallace could not turn down offers from kings. That kind of thing just could not be done then. And King Edward especially was not the kind of man that you could refuse. Wallace knew this. This insult to what King Edward would regard as his generosity was enough to rule out any peaceful end to Wallace's story. Since Wallace could not be bought, the King was left with only one other answer to his Wallace problem – kill him.

After Falkirk, Wallace still had the support of the Church and the common people. He still had an army even though it was smaller. But things were not the same. It was time for a change. Wallace decided, or was persuaded, that Scotland's cause would best be served by him taking on some other role and leaving the direct running of the country to the nobles. So he resigned his position as Guardian. Three new ones were appointed. They continued the fight against King Edward.

Had Wallace failed then? Many have thought that he had, pointing to the defeat at Falkirk and his resignation later on. But I feel that he had not failed. You see, England was too big and too rich for Scotland to win back her freedom with a good summer's fighting.

The war would have to be one of endurance. Success for the Scots would lie in keeping faith with their cause, hanging in, rolling with the punches and getting up from a big knockdown. In this way they would wear the English down. It is in the nurturing of this spirit and in the practical measures he took to keep the struggle alive that we have to judge Wallace's success. Scotland did not fall to pieces into King Edward's lap. Even the fickle nobles did not all rush to make peace with the English. Who could have done better than Wallace?

Three months after Falkirk, King Edward left Scotland. Some castles and towns had been captured from the Scots but, apart from this, he had gained no real benefit from his invasion and victory. Scotland was still proud and free.

Wallace Abroad

Although a Scot, Wallace would
also have regarded himself as a
European

For nearly a year after Falkirk we do not know what
Wallace was doing. Although he was not in the
Guardian's hot seat any more, he would still have been
busy. This was because Scottish pressure was mounting
at the Pope's court in Rome to make King Edward
release King John. There was a chance that some deal
could be done that would allow King John to return to
Scotland. Such a deal depended on Scottish unity.

Wallace was probably busy using his considerable prestige and following to ensure that the different groups in Scotland would unite firmly behind King John when he was released.

You might think in this time that Wallace would have set his heart on punishing those responsible for the desertion of the Scottish cavalry at Falkirk. But whatever happened at Falkirk, Wallace would have to live with it. He would not want to risk stirring up a civil war by starting to blame and punish people. He knew that it was necessary to stay friendly with the nobles for both political and military reasons. Sure, Wallace could bring an army into the field, but without reliable cavalry it would get shot down by archers just like at Falkirk. It was the nobles who controlled the cavalry. And it was them that ultimately controlled King John's destiny. Wallace's best hope for a free Scotland with her own king returned would be to maintain his independent force in battle readiness and keep friendly with the nobles working for King John's return. Even though they were not always reliable in Scotland's cause, things simply could not be done without the nobles.

The Vatican arranged King John's release in the summer of 1299. But he was not free to come back to Scotland. Scotland herself was still free of English domination, but the situation with the Guardians was very tense and uncertain. In fact, two of the Guardians, Bruce and Comyn, both contenders for King John's empty throne, had been brawling with each other at a meeting in Peebles.

It was a delicate time and Scotland needed as many friends abroad as it could get. Friends that could provide money for the army, provisions and weapons, political support and put diplomatic pressure on King Edward.

The job of finding this support could only be given to one man, Wallace. Just around the time of King John's release, Wallace left for the Continent of Europe with the full support of the Guardians, the Church and the people. He was going to be away for some time, at least a year. We can be sure that this must have pleased quite a few people inside Scotland as well as some outside it.

In Wallace's day the connection to Europe was strong and Wallace would have thought of himself as a European and a Scot. He must have been excited at the prospect of visiting the cultural centre of his world in mainland Europe and seeing the large and prosperous cities he would have heard merchants and bishops speak of since the days of his childhood. In the Scotland of his day there were many family ties to France, Holland and Flanders and this would have added an extra personal interest to his journeys. He would have seen riches that would have made his eyes pop. He would have been fêted and dined by kings and barons and bishops. He would have been treated with the greatest sympathy and respect. But, at the same time, there was always the danger of an assassin's dagger or a treacherous host seeking favour or reward from King Edward.

Worst of all, Wallace would have found that all the kind words counted for nothing. Scotland would have to struggle alone against England. France would help, but only when it suited the French. To say this is not to blame the French – they were sincere in their desire to help Scotland. But they too were faced with a debilitating war against England. And the reality was that Scotland was just a pawn in the big struggle between England and France. And Scotland might be saved or sacrificed as it suited them.

Wallace came back home a wiser and sadder man. He knew now that there was no way of ending the war except by grimly fighting on and on and on. And gradually grinding down King Edward's desire to hold Scotland. The spilling of English blood was the only answer. It would be a war in which everyone would lose.

Wallace might have returned by the summer of 1301 and taken part in Bruce's campaign to clear the English from the South-West of Scotland. He might have taken part in the Battle of Roslin on February 24th, 1303 in which the Scots surprised a large English force and sorely punished it. But the first definite knowledge we have of his presence back home is in June 1303, when he took part in a minor campaign in South-West Scotland and Cumberland. This was designed to divert the English from their own campaign in Scotland by sending troops to defend these areas. It did not work. And King Edward had his most successful campaign ever. It looked as if Scotland was just too small to win against England, Europe's mightiest country.

The Scots were in a sorry state now. In the five years since the defeat at Falkirk, they had continued to fight bravely. But with the failure to get their own king back and in the absence of solid support from abroad they were running out of steam.

Then came the big blow. In May 1303, the English signed a peace treaty with the French. The Scots were truly on their own now. King Edward would be able to bring back from France all the tough soldiers that had been fighting there. He would now be able to crush Scotland. More and more people were realising that all the years of failure had hardened his determination to rule Scotland. The Scots nobles now knew that they were in a situation in which they either surrendered or lost everything. The English King had finally worn them down. He would have Scotland or he would totally destroy it. This was the choice.

In the end what the Scots wanted did not matter. You have to make peace with the victor. A general surrender was finally agreed on 9th February, 1304. King Edward had Scotland in his pocket. The people that refused to surrender were declared traitors to Scotland and its lawful ruler, King Edward of England. And chief of the traitors, in the King's book, was William Wallace.

Scots speak about their future

THE HARD YEAR

If ever Wallace needed courage it
was now

With all around you capitulating or captured or dead, it would take an iron will to hang on to your beliefs. Wallace was such a man. Like his adversary King Edward, he was the sort of man who kept on going until it was all over. This was a time to be flexible, to nod your head and smile and keep your plans in the dark. Wallace had too much pride to do this. Many would regard his stand as pig-headed. It is not difficult to accept that this point of view is a valid one.

Wallace still had many of the common people behind him and the Church too, but the real power now lay with the nobles. And they, once again, were being cautious. Secret plans were definitely being plotted, but they could sit on ice until the right moment. You have to remember that each person had their own idea of what was best for Scotland and what was the best way to achieve it. In the fight for Scotland's freedom it's not always possible to point a finger and say what is right from wrong. Wallace is Scotland's great patriot, but that does not mean that he was always right or that everyone had to agree with him. Wallace's constant warfare approach just did not work with a man like King Edward. It was necessary to make compromises and accept that King John's hopes of regaining the Scottish throne were finished. The nobles were more able to accept the reality of Scotland's situation, but Wallace and his friends could not.

There comes a time for all leaders when they are rejected. Wallace was no exception. The qualities that made him great were seen as impediments to the progress of the cause. Times change. The hard man, the iron will, the inspiring leader of 1297 was not the right leader for the more flexible times that had followed. Wallace was not a flexible man.

He was now a wanted outlaw with a price on his head. Above all the other 'rebels' King Edward wanted Wallace. All sorts of people were after him, from ruthless bounty hunters to old friends that had been held to ransom. Wallace had already had a couple of close escapes from capture or assassination. And many would have rued the day that they set out with Wallace's head as their aim.

By late 1304 the pressure was on. Gangs were scouring the country with the sole object of getting him. A couple of times they came near to it. Wallace, though, had not lost his skill with the sword nor his instinct for survival. Although Wallace could still have commanded a large force, this would only draw attention to himself. He would best stay free by travelling alone or with a few companions. Sometimes he would have lived rough, other times he would stay with old friends and supporters. This would be a time when his hand was always on his dirk.

Every place a trap, everyone a potential traitor, around every corner an ambush. It must have been a very tired Wallace that was finally captured by the Scottish knight, Sir John Menteith at Robroyston near Glasgow on 3rd of August 1305. We do not know why he was there. We do not know who was with him. We do not know what the documents he had with him contained.

To prevent any rescue attempt he was immediately whisked off to England, arriving in London on August 22nd. The very next day he was taken to hear of the crimes he had committed against England and her King. Wallace's only recorded words during the trial were to forcefully deny that he was a traitor to Scotland or to King Edward, for he had never sworn an oath of loyalty to him. His claims made no difference. Wallace was told of his sentence. He could hardly have been surprised by it.

We can imagine him hearing of his fearful fate with a brave face. He was to be hanged, disembowelled, beheaded and cut into quarters that were going to be sent all over the country as a warning to any others who might think of rebelling.

Wallace was dragged through the streets of London, packed with jeering crowds. We can be sure that he faced his terrible death with the dignity befitting a hero. Blind Harry tells us that Wallace had a request – that at the moment of death he be allowed to read his old prayer book. This was granted to him by Clifford, an old English soldier and rival from the war. He was executed with his eyes fixed on the book held before him by a priest.

Wallace's chopped-off limbs were sent to Scotland. But King Edward's warning did not work and the year was not out before Robert the Bruce made himself King of Scots and raised another rebellion. A rebellion that after long hard years of campaigns, battles, hardship and courage wrestled back Scottish independence.

OUR MAN

The story does not end with Wallace's execution, just the first part of it

Wallace showed the Scots what was possible if they kept faith with their vision of a free Scotland and were prepared, each one of them, to face the consequences of that belief. His message was that their destiny as a people lies in their own hands.

It is easy to believe in things that do not really matter. But what makes Scots people distinctive is the ability to stand up for things they know to be true, even though they will have to take a blow for it. Such a people were their ancestors.

They proved, despite what some historians have believed, that people then did care about their country and its right to independence. But that right had to be won from England and against the hardest of English kings. Victory could only be achieved by a tremendous unity and sacrifice by all the people in Scotland regardless of their wealth, title or job.

In the dark days it was Wallace who came forward. Wallace believed in his country and in its people and their freedom. He put himself on the line for it, and for the Scottish people since. He's dead, but his story does not end there and neither does Scotland's. For we carry all that pain and courage in our heads and in our hearts. As long as we live, as long as Scotland is still searching for freedom, Wallace is with us in our heads and always true in our hearts.

Glossary
of some Unfamiliar Words

bickering	constantly disagreeing
burghers	leading citizens and town officials
canny	careful, very aware of one's own interests
Celtic	the ancient European tribal culture and language which exerted its greatest influence on Scotland and Ireland
chain-mail	armour made of interconnected metal
crossbow bolt	a short heavy arrow
dirk	a very large knife
Flanders	an ancient country which straddled modern Belgium and Holland
lairds	landowners, lesser lords
loch	a lake
peat	a fuel cut from bogs
put to the sword	slaughtered
schiltroms	massed regiments of spearmen up to 1000 strong
Scots language	an ancient variety of the English tongue that developed in Scotland
succour	give help in time of need

William Wallace – a Scots life

SCOTS LANGUAGE EDITION

1 874640 46 7 £6.99

This Scots language edition of *William Wallace – a Scots life* was first published in 1995 and has run to three printings. Originally conceived for younger and new readers in Scots, this volume successfully launched the Scots legends series. These are short but well-researched life stories of figures who have achieved heroic status from past and present-day Scotland.

For information on these and other titles from Argyll Publishing, send for a catalogue to:

Argyll Publishing
Glendaruel
Argyll PA22 3AE
tel 01369 820229

"every Scots schoolkid should have one"
West Coast Magazine

"... a breakthrough"
Chapman

"... instill(s) pride and a knowledge of Scotland's national heroes in the country's youth"
Celtic Heritage

Robert the Bruce
– a Scots life

SCOTS LANGUAGE EDITION
1 874640 52 1 £6.99

No man was more deserving of recognition as a hero than Robert the Bruce. His life can be viewed rightly as a triumph of will, guile and courage. Like his contemporary William Wallace, the story of his life is intimately connected to Scotland's struggle for survival.

This sympathetic but critical account for younger and new readers in Scots is the first book on Bruce to be written in that language since Barbour's *Brus* in 1376.

"readable, accessible to young and old"
The Herald

"entirely successful"
Billy Kay, Cencrastus

"... retelling really important parts of Scottish history with great panache"
Robbie Robertson,
Asst Director
Scottish Consultative
Curriculum Council

**Jock Stein
– a Scots life**

SCOTS LANGUAGE EDITION

1 874640 13 0 £6.99

From humble beginnings in the Lanarkshire coalfield, Jock Stein became one of the most successful Scots of his generation. Under his leadership, Celtic became an awesome force in Scottish football and were the first British club to win the European Cup. He later achieved success as manager of the Scotland international team.

Written in easy-to-read modern Scots, Glenn Telfer's biography explores the connection between Stein's working class upbringing and his emergence as a cultural figure of immense significance.

"an enjoyable biography"
Scots Magazine

"an essential part of any fan's collection"
Celtic View

"Glenn Telfer's succint biography does justice to one of the most unlikely of Scotland's cultural icons"

Education Herald